Caroline Rowland

French Charm

How to Open Doors Anywhere in the World

Illustrations:
Cover, "Homework," and "Table" by Patrick Texier
All other illustrations by Lionelle Daudel

Back cover: Photograph by Henry Kwok

Cover and book design: Korongo Graphics
36 Highland Avenue, Randolph VT 05060
korongotex@aol.com

Edited by Sara Tucker

ISBN-13: 978-1494243180
ISBN-10: 1494243180

Contents

French Charm

All doors open to courtesy.

—THOMAS FULLER

Introduction

My name is Caroline. I was raised in France in a family that insisted on good manners and the respect of etiquette. Of course, as a child, I resisted these lessons as much as I could, behaving when my parents were around and joyfully breaking the rules when they were away. Yet the lessons sank in, one way or another, and many years later, after having lived in many countries, I discovered that there was one thing you could take with you everywhere, that has no weight (I do so love to travel light), does not cost you any money, and will open more doors than you can imagine, allowing you to make friends with people of all cultures, languages, and backgrounds: manners.

Unfortunately, manners seem to be rapidly disappearing in today's society. I was in New York not long ago, and a man held the door for me. I looked him in the eyes and thanked him — and he actually thanked me for thanking him! Apparently, the woman before me had not even acknowledged his gesture — probably the same woman who will later say that men are not gentlemen anymore.

If you are like me — living fast, always on the go, a bit of a maverick — it is impossible to remember every single rule. And that is okay.

When I graduated from university, I went to spend one year in England. While there, I was invited to a party in a castle. Not knowing the rules of the game in this part of the world and having definitely never been invited to a real castle before, I was quite nervous, but mercifully, my training took over. I went to my default mode—"proper and polite"—and they apparently still think that I was raised in a castle somewhere in the south of France. I did not think about what to do or what not to do; after all, I was there to enjoy the moment. I just let the old upbringing come back, and I did feel like a princess, castle or not.

I have lived in Europe, Africa, Turkey, and the United States, and each time I changed countries and cultures, what saved me from embarrassment and helped me make real friends and find work were good manners. It won't get you the job, but it will do a great job opening the doors for you.

I have worked as an interpreter, and I have seen more social blunders that tipped the balance the wrong way than you can imagine. If you want to sell something, the last thing you want to do is irritate your client. Put him at ease; treat him like a king!

Like many girls in New York, I've had my fair share of dates after which I could not wait to run back home, call my girlfriends, and the conversation would inevitably start: "You won't believe what he did!" The most disastrous dates are the best ones for a laugh. But the man who pays attention — he's the one you remember, the one for whom you will check your phone constantly.

So there are many good books out there on etiquette, books that deal with the subject in depth, sometimes even disagreeing with each other. What I have written is a brief summary of the main rules, short and sweet, for those who have neither the time nor the patience to thumb through a hefty book. If you just want to have the main points covered, this is the book for you.

My friend Sara was telling me that when she took care of her mother that it was the most enriching, wonderful experience for her, something that she did not expect, at least not to that extent. I believe that when you put others first, you actually put yourself first. What I mean is that — if only for just a moment — you are the knight, the gentleman in the room, or the princess, the lady in the party. And the feeling is so ingratiating that by just little adjustments, you have transformed your evening into a night worthy of an A. Dumas novel, you have recreated yourself and the evening.

Politeness is the flower of humanity.

—JOSEPH JOUBERT

1

Philosophy

The basis of etiquette—of impressing people at a social event, a professional gathering, or on a date —is simple. You do not need to be the smartest, the richest, or the most beautiful person in the room. In fact, you can easily steal the flame from them by just one little thing: When others tread on toes and egos, you will be the one whose awareness saves the day! Think of good manners as a French fashion statement: It is all in the details, the subtlety, and the understated refinement of a foulard, the whiff of a mysterious perfume that will never be forgotten.

And remember, to be gallant is not a set of rules; it is a way of being, a default mode that you have installed in your personal programming.

Too many rules to remember? Practice makes perfect. Practice at home, on your own, or with friends, so that good manners become a reflex. After a while the rules will become second nature and you will look comfortable following them. Remember how you felt the first time you wore a suit? You want to avoid that feeling. Practice, have fun with it.

Think of the following prescriptions not as rules but as guidelines. You will find yourself in situations where they do not apply, confronting unforeseen events, but if you understand the idea behind the rules, you'll be fine. Use your brain and common sense and ask yourself this question: "What would be a dignified way to show I care?" It's that simple.

Let's start.

No matter where you are, it is your social obligation to make everyone feel comfortable around you, no matter what their social status is. It is by adapting that you prove yourself as a person of education. Be respectful to all, in a detached way: There is a balance between being subservient and arrogant. Be mindful of others before your own needs. Just make sure you are clear what those needs are. Do not assume anything; get all the info before acting.

The safest and surest way to be invited again and again is to make your interlocutors shine. That should be more important for you than showing off. Whether man or woman, make them feel that they are the most interesting person in the world and let them shine in front of all. But do avoid obvious flattery and superficial compliments; they have probably heard it all before, lots. As for you, give a glimpse of your light, and let them fish for it. You are so great that you have no need to show it, just entice their curiosity and they will be excited to discover it.

When not to accept an invitation: We are not talking about marriage here ("In sickness and good health . . ."), so if you are feeling down, whether physically or emotionally, call your closest friends and stay home. Do not go to an event and share your miseries with people who are trying to have a good time; they will resent you for it and justifiably run away from you, which will only add to your misery.

2

Order, Please!

At a formal gathering, as a general rule, the host opens the ceremony. Introductions proceed in the following order (you may have to do some research on who is who— Viva Google!):

- Women before men
- Older before younger
- Members of the clergy first, then military, then civil
- A first-time guest over usual ones
- A foreigner over a native
- A guest of honor before others.

When you are introduced to an older person or one of higher rank, wait for him (or her) to extend his hand. If he doesn't, a polite nod of the head is the appropriate gesture. Do not presume to shake hands with every person to whom you are introduced; body language will let you know which way to go.

When a new person arrives, it is common for the men in the room to stand up, especially if the newcomer is a woman. The men may have to remain standing till the ladies sit down. That may mean that as a man you are getting quite an aerobic workout if ladies keep coming in and out of the room.

Let the most important people in the room have the last word on any subject, whether you agree with them or not. It is not your job to prove them wrong or to steal the show.

3

Walking, Climbing, Entering, Exiting

When two men and a woman are walking, going in or out of a public place, the men should surround her: one in the front and one on the side, for example; or they should place themselves between the woman and where there are the most people. As a general rule, the man will walk on the dangerous side for safety reasons (nearest the road, for example).

In a stairway, the man precedes the woman when they go down the stairs and follows her when

As a general rule, the man will walk on the
dangerous side for safety reasons.

they go up. Again, it is common sense: He places himself so that he can prevent or arrest a fall.

When entering a place, a gentleman will let the ladies enter first, except when entering a public place such as a bar or a restaurant. This custom is a holdover from ancient times, when the man was supposed to check the place to make sure it was safe. Be careful, though, for some ladies do not know about that rule and may assume that you should always let them in first, no matter what. (If they complain, just give them this book and mark the page.)

Of course, doors are the gentleman's responsibility, but if he has to exit first (from an elevator, for instance), he should hold the door for the women. Ladies, do not forget to thank the people who are acting with such *délicatesse* — or if you do not, do not be surprised the next time a door is slammed on you!

Caroline Rowland

In a stairway, the man precedes the woman
when they go down . . .

11

. . . and follows her when they go up.

Il a la politesse du coeur, bien supérieure à celle des manières.

—J. BARTHÉLÉMY

4

"Baise-main"

Unless you are royalty, this practice —
employed when you're introduced to a
person of high rank — is generally
reserved for indoors. The man bends to
apparently kiss the hand (he should just
slightly brush over), and should never
raise the hand to him.

Never raise the lady's hand to your lips.

5

Staff

Respect the members of your host's staff, no matter where you are. Remember that they are not your employees, and you are not their boss. Greet the staff with a hello and a smile — that's it — and ask them politely for what you need. Do not be overfriendly; to do so could put your host in an embarrassing situation. If you need to talk to a member of the personnel, do so discreetly; long, drawn-out conversations with staff members will only embarrass them or your host. Never clap your hands or snap your fingers to get their attention! Remember that they are the staff of your hosts, not yours (unless you are ready to take over their salaries), and that to be rude to the personnel is to be rude to your host. If they have taken good care of you, leave a generous tip in cash.

6

Body Language

Eyes: Eye contact depends on the culture. In some countries, you must look straight into the eyes of the person you're talking to, but in other countries it is a sign of arrogance. Do your homework and check.

Mouth: Don't keep your lips closed tight, a sign of nervousness, or let your mouth hang open (the flies in the room may not be so tasty); neither habit will add to your charm.

Body position: Straight and straight and straight again (work on it; good posture will do fabulous things for your back and stomach). Don't, however, look contrived or as if you were sitting on a stick — you must always look comfortable, even if you are not. Legs should not be wide open whether standing or sitting, especially sitting. I am sure you have better parts of yourself to show! Crossing of the legs, however, while usually acceptable for women, is less appropriate for men, especially at the table or in an official place. (But crossing of the legs for men is a very effective way to hide certain overenthusiastic body responses.)

Posture and movement: Be light and silent and delicate in all circumstances. If you do not know

17

what to do with your hands, clasp them behind you or over your chest, or just grab a glass of wine.

Clothes: The number-one requirement of good grooming, for both men and women, is to be clean and neat. Even your "cool" look must be neat. Much will be forgiven when it comes to style, but cleanliness is an absolute must. Beyond that, your look should be neither too sober nor too colorful; play it safe. Make sure that your clothes are comfortable, very comfortable, or you will suffer the whole evening.

7

Clothes Off

When entering a house or a church, men should remove their hat or cap, as well as gloves and sunglasses.

When introduced, men should take the right glove off to shake hands; women may leave theirs on.

As an overnight guest at a party, make sure you know what activities will be offered so that you can bring the appropriate clothes. A bathing suit should provide appropriate coverage—a string bikini or a Speedo might not be the best choice. Whatever the setting, cover everything that should be covered. If you're unsure, long sleeves are usually the safest choice. Ties must fit shirts or vice versa. Tuck shirts in pants. Avoid letting your undershirt show.

You must look elegantly natural, even if it took you hours to look so. Avoid overpowering perfume or cologne. If the weather is in the nineties and the occasion calls for a jacket, make it a light one: You may have to wait a long time in the sweltering heat before the host invites you to take it off.

8

Conversation

Develop the art of small talk; it is the art of the superfluous. When running out of things to say, try the question game, for rare is the person who does not like to talk about himself—and do try to look alert and interested (could be tricky). Before an event, if conversation is not your forte, read some articles on art, on the latest bestseller, etc. Vacation is always a good topic, a tale you may enrich a little; do not let reality cramp your style. The weather, if not original, is at least a safe topic.

Remember the art of the exclamation: "How wonderful! How surprising! Fabulous!" Try not to make it sound clichéd, though. And don't say, "How interesting" unless you mean it. Politeness that lacks sincerity becomes a form of insult.

Work on your vocabulary and grammar if those were the classes you avoided at school. And of course, do not swear—a sure sign of a very limited vocabulary.

Do not use *he* or *she* when the person whom you are talking about is present; use the person's name—not "She went to Paris" but "Patricia went to Paris."

Speaking of which, it's also a good idea to make mental notes of people's titles; some have worked their whole life for them.

Be a good listener, show interest, and ask questions (do not transform yourself into a detective, though). If you feel stuck, a good trick is to repeat the last part of the sentence, the word or the phrase, in a questioning tone: "I just came back from Tokyo." "Tokyo?!" The speaker will usually add something without being prompted. Be careful not to be caught, though, by being too obvious about it.

When asked how you are, remember, you are doing great (even if you feel miserable). People get together to enjoy themselves, relax, laugh, and not to hear about your problems; they have enough of their own.

As a host or a guest, it is your duty to participate in the conversation, but be careful not to monopolize it; this is not your stage. Be careful when telling a funny anecdote or a joke; this is not a question of being politically correct, but of showing *délicatesse* toward everybody. Do not make jokes at the expense of someone else; it will come back to them and return to you tenfold. Avoid saying anything bad about anyone: Words have a strange way of traveling to their victim, who will find their source more easily than you think.

No matter what, do not look bored; it will not make you look superior, just snobbish. Since you may have to go through a few very boring parties, you may have to pull on your acting skills a lot.

Do not talk about money if you are at a party; people will resent you for bringing them back to office talk. You are here to enjoy yourself and impress.

Other topics to avoid: religion (you are entitled to your own beliefs and so are others), politics, sex, and business. There may be an exception for the latter, just be subtle about it.

Magic words: *Thank you, please, you're welcome* — it is impossible to overuse these.

Learn a few words of the local language: *please, thank you, hello,* and so on.

If you're placed in a confrontational situation with no way out, choose murderous silence; it is much more effective and ever so much more frustrating to others. Learn to divert a conversation when it is getting heated. Your host will be grateful for that. If a person is being rude, you may want to save the evening, the atmosphere, and the party by changing the topic or giving an opportunity for the person under fire to leave the conversation.

Have to make a speech? Make it short and entertaining for everybody.

Do not talk (or walk, for that matter) too fast or you will lose half of your audience; too slow, on the other hand, and you will put them to sleep.

Restrooms: Leave the other occupants in peace. This is not the right place to engage in conversation. It is the "time out" zone! People will appreciate your discretion in allowing everyone to take a break from socializing for a while.

9

Pay Attention

If you are on a date, or just having a good time with a special friend, do not spend the evening checking out the people around you. Your companion has probably spent considerable time and money to look their best for you; the least you can do is to show respect by acting as a gentleman or as a lady. If you are more interested in other people, fine, but do not waste the time of someone else.

For the seating arrangement, always leave the more comfortable seat or the one with the best view to the woman or the guest of honor.

10

Answer Always

Always respond to an invitation, whether it is to accept or decline. In the latter case, you may want to give a reason, even if it is a vague one. Be careful, though, for if you refuse an invitation twice, it may be interpreted as your not wanting to be with the people who invited you at all. Once invited, it is customary to return the invitation; even if you declined, you are not off the hook. What counts is that you were invited.

Always send a thank-you note, or a letter if you were an overnight guest. What should you say? It must not be a basic thank-you card. Take this opportunity to praise the quality of the welcome you received, the beauty of the place where you stayed, of its surroundings, the joy of some of the conversation you had. Feel free to add some charming anecdotes that happened that evening. Make it personal.

Always respond to an invitation and later send a personalized thank-you note—NOT a basic card.

Courtesy is as much a mark of a gentleman as courage.
—THEODORE ROOSEVELT

11

Telephone

At the table, put your cellular on vibrate
or choose a discreet ring. No one should have to
hear your conversation. If you absolutely must take
a call, excuse yourself from the table.

Speak softly when you are on your cellular in
public.

If you change lines, do not leave your
interlocutor waiting too long. Tell the second
person you will call him right back.

When calling someone at home, and especially if
it is the spouse who answers, immediately say who
you are and maybe the reason for your call. Then,
and then only, ask for the person you want to talk to.

Do not call people too early or too late, at lunch
or dinnertime, during rest time or family time.

12

Homework

If possible, get information on the people you are going to meet—their names, jobs, hobbies, as well as their taboo subjects.

13

Traps

An itch? Too bad. Excuse yourself, find a place alone, or endure.

State your opinions, for they are yours, but do not go into combat—most people who attack your beliefs are probably not worth your time and energy. Leave confrontation to those who are insecure. You are above a dispute; use indifference, a "not worth my time" attitude. A grand sense of humor works, too.

Sneezing, coughing, yawning, burping, and other annoying mishaps must be done facing away from people and as silently and discreetly as possible. Leave the room if it seems that you are going to be hit by a big one; you will feel better and so will the people around you. If it is your interlocutor who sneezes or has another mishap, ignore it the first time (they will appreciate your not bringing attention to it), but if it happens again, hard to ignore, feel free to offer the appropriate formulas of politeness.

If someone is in an embarrassing situation (a piece of food in their teeth, a fly opened), try to make him or her aware of it discreetly, in undercover terms. If they do not get it, you did your duty, let it go.

14

Time Is of the Essence

If you are late, call. For a woman, fifteen minutes is acceptable; more is rude, and then do apologize for your lateness. Men should be on time.

Time to leave: Conventionally, around one hour after dinner is over and coffee is served. Earlier would be rude—did you come only for the food? Later is imposing on your hosts. Again, you have to use common sense: If the party keeps going, stay. If the guests start leaving, take the hint. And if your host starts offering juices, take the second hint.

15

Entrance/Exit

At a large gathering, find your hosts and say hello when you arrive. Search them out again and say good-bye before leaving.

For a woman, fifteen minutes late is
acceptable. Men should be on time.

16

Table

Before sitting at the table, be sure to visit the restrooms, **wash your hands,** and make sure that you are presentable. If necessary, loosen your belt one knot so that you can be comfortable (you will be thankful later on that you did).

Never do anything before your host does it first. That means do not start eating, drinking, dancing, even engaging in table conversation before given the go signal. If your host did not read that book and seems to have forgotten about his or her starving guests, you can bring the attention back to the food in a subtle manner, by showing appreciation and interest. You are expected to taste all the dishes: if you have allergies, your host should have taken note of it. If he hasn't, avoid the food in a discreet manner.

If you have a designated seat at a table, you must stay there and cannot change it. Usually, a great deal of planning has gone into the seating arrangement; you do not want to ruin hours of work. If you are the host, make sure you also know about your guests' peculiarities.

Sit up straight but relaxed, and be sure not to bother the people sitting next to you with your elbows, or in front of you with your feet. Do not put your forearm on the table either. Before speaking or drinking — or kissing — always make sure your mouth is empty. Never speak with your mouth full, and *never* chew with your mouth open. Chew silently — practice at home in front of a mirror.

If you have something in your teeth that is really bothering you, excuse yourself and go to the bathroom. If you are stuck at the table, time to start playing magician with your napkin.

Dinner conversation: Do not speak too loud (everybody around you is entitled to their own conversation) or so low that your interlocutor has to bend over the table or ask you to repeat what you are saying over and over.

Make sure that the right order in the conversation is followed (that means respect hierarchy). You must equally pay attention to the person sitting at your left and the one at your right. When speaking, turn your head toward the person you're addressing — but not your whole body, for that would be rude to the person on the other side, who would suddenly have a back facing them. If you must talk to someone far from you, you may want to wait till you are closer to them and start maneuvering as soon as the guests leave the table.

Duties: It is a good idea for men to learn how to open bottles of wine and Champagne, to cut meat, and to open oysters. You may be given the honor. Cutting meat is the host's work or for the guest of honor, so be ready. It is also "gentleman's work" to make sure that the glasses of the ladies next to him are full.

I do what with what? When a dish is presented to you, you must take the pieces the closer to you: do not choose another piece nor turn the plate. And remember that the best piece is usually reserved for the guest of honor. When passing a plate, make sure the utensils do not fall into the dish and that they are placed toward the next person to be served.

Utensils: If you do not know which utensils to use, start with those farthest from your plate and work your way in (good manners are always, or at least most of the time, based on common sense).

– If you have any doubt about whether you should use utensils or not, watch your neighbors.

– Never put your silverware back on the table after you've used it: the tablecloth is often made of an expensive material. Besides, you do not want your corner of the table to be the only dirty one, which may result in your spending the next dinner party at the kids' table.

– Forks on the left, spoons and knives on your right.

– When you eat, be elegant about it; you need not stab your food unless it is alive and appears to want to make a run for it. Hold the end of the handles. Be careful with the silverware, it may very well be a family heirloom.

– Too much silverware? Do not panic, they may just be for show.

– When you've finished eating, leave your fork and knife on your plate, or place the knife on the *pose-couteaux* if there is one. How you position your utensils depends on the country, so if you're unsure, watch your neighbor.

Remember that you are not invited to stuff yourself and/or get drunk. No matter how good the food is, **do not overindulge,** and do not serve yourself again unless invited to do so first (if you are a host, it is your duty to invite your guests to have more and to be aware of who is done with his plate or glass).

How to Eat

Food will be served on your left, drinks on your right, but plates will be taken on your right.

– The food goes to your mouth, not the opposite: to avoid spilling, take small pieces.

– It is not of good taste to start by putting the pieces you do not like on the side of your plate.

– When you are cutting, whether bread or cheese, always cut small slices or pieces.

– Never take the last piece, unless absolutely coerced by the host.

– Enjoy the delicacies you are offered *as they are served*. Do not ask for ice in your glass of wine or ketchup for your beefsteak. You must eat food the way it is served. You are not in a restaurant.

Soup: Do not put the whole spoon in your mouth. The spoon goes to your mouth in a perpendicular way and you let the liquid flow naturally. No slurping. No scraping the bottom of the bowl.

Cheese: You must cut a little piece of cheese — put the tray on the table if you have to. Do not only take the inside of the cheese. If you are presented with a platter of six cheeses, for example, you can go up to three pieces. Put a small piece of cheese on a small piece of bread and enjoy. When you're done with the cheese knife, you may have to clean it on your plate so that the next person does not get a taste of your choices.

Avoid pastas: If you are in a restaurant and want to impress, you may want to avoid pastas — many of them are messy to eat. If you do order them, try to roll a few pieces around your fork, with the help of your spoon if necessary. Avoid the knife, the sucking noise, and the splashing of sauce all over. Quite a test of ability. Just as a rule, avoid hard-to-eat or smelly food.

Caviar: Take a few grains with your knife and put them on a small piece of bread. If served with cream or other ingredients, use your fork.

Foie gras: Take with your fork and follow with bread — you can put some on the bread directly but *do not spread it.*

36

Asparagus: Cut the spears with your fork, not with your knife.

Fruits: These may have to be cut using your fork and knife. My advice, go for the fruit salad unless you are an expert, or you may see your fruit flying through the room.

Leftovers stay on your plate, never on the table. To know whether you should finish your plate completely or leave a little, take your cue from your host.

If you drop something: Take immediate action for damage control and do not make a bit fuss about it; it is an incident, not a drama.

Refills: If you want more wine, finish your glass. If you do not wish for more, make sure to leave some in your glass.

Opening a bottle of wine is still considered a man's job. And remember that as a guest, you may be given the honor to taste the wine, so you may want to learn how to do so. When pouring, do not hold the bottle from underneath; only waiters do that, so their client can see the label.

Breakfast: A "Good morning, ladies and gentlemen" suffices first thing in the morning. Do not feel obligated to start a whole conversation: it is one of the rare meals when people may just want to relax, be quiet, give time for their body to wake up, read the newspaper, and so on.

Sharing a dish in a restaurant: Ask for an extra plate and divide the food before touching it.

At a buffet: Dip before biting a piece of food, and do not dip the same piece twice. You can also put some of the sauce on your plate.

17

Biz-date Lunch or Dinner

If you're the host, propose a few different dates, confirm the day before, and see if you can arrange to pick up your guests. If not, meet them at the restaurant, but be sure to arrive first.

Propose a few different restaurants, and make sure you know them — the noise level, the quality of food and service, and so on.

The guest of honor gets the best seat, and the host is usually seated with his back to the room.

If there is one, provide your guests with a menu without price.

If you know the restaurant, you can recommend some specialties, but you must let the other person order what and how much they want.

Order wine with the meal.

If you are the host, follow the lead of your guests: If they order appetizers, do so. If they want a dessert, so do you — even if you take just a few bites. You want your guest to feel comfortable eating. But of course, use reason and common sense: whether a guest or the host, do not automatically choose the most expensive items on the menu, nor eat or drink too much.

The host leads the conversation, but wait till all your guests have ordered and settled down to introduce the topic of the day.

Do not draw out lunch meetings; use the "I have an appointment" excuse not to spend the whole day at the restaurant: your wallet and your waistline will thank you for it.

Ask for the bill and pay discreetly. If you are a guest, do not forget to thank your host.

If the lunch or dinner is a date, rather than a business engagement, ladies should have the elegance to eat the food that they have ordered. Follow your diet another day, or make sure you order what you can eat. A bonus: People will think that you are just naturally slim.

Makeup touchup? Do not do it at the table. Excuse yourself and go to the ladies' room.

At the end of the dinner, do not forget to thank your host with a charming smile, even if you cannot wait to get out of there. And gentlemen, call the next day to thank the lady for her company.

Be sure you know the restaurant you propose—
noise level, quality of food and service, etc.

18

Drinking

Wine is preferable to beer at a social gathering, but make sure you know your limits—that is, how many drinks you can allow yourself and still be alert, aware, funny, entertaining, and polite.

Coffee: Never leave the spoon inside the cup; put it back on the saucer.

Hold your glass at the bottom, not underneath.

Make sure the lady's glass is always full.

Fill a wine glass halfway; water and champagne, full glass.

Remember: Getting drunk will make you both a fool and an undesirable guest. You may also pass a good opportunity to shine, especially when the competition has already collapsed shamefully on the nearest sofa, drunk!

19

Dancing

It is your duty to invite the hostess to dance. Thank your partner after the dance.

20

Let's Play

It is a good idea to learn a sport, a game ... be a good sport, no matter what. Remain calm and appreciative of your partner. If necessary, you may let your opponent win, in a subtle way, if you think it would be a treat for him.

21

Sleeping

As an overnight guest in someone's home or a hotel, make sure that you follow the "no noise" rule (unless you wish to never be invited again).

If you share a bedroom, change clothes in another room, and do not take over the whole place, the blankets, etc.

Make sure you have decent nightclothes and house clothes, and before meeting people for breakfast, wash first.

22

Love

There is a huge difference but only a fine line between being charming, which will put you in the good graces of all, and flirting, which is bound to bring forth the jealousy or the ire of others. When addressing the opposite sex in a business or formal setting, avoid verbal compliments that might lead to confusion, misinterpretation, and proof of a total lack of manners.

No one mentions another person's love life. If you see two people behaving in ways that suggest a liaison, say nothing! Always give them the benefit of the doubt, even if there is no doubt; a gentleman just does not notice certain things.

Do not flirt or check out the guests during ceremonies. This is extremely disrespectful to the people who invited you. Wait till you are outside.

For couples: If you are not married, you may end up in separate bedrooms when invited to stay over. Accept it. And if the fun and the excitement of wandering in the corridors at night are too irresistible, make sure you are not caught, that you are going to the right room, and that you are back in your own room before breakfast. If the bed has been unused, muss the sheets, for the sake of appearance—a form of delicate politeness.

If you are not married . . .

. . . you may end up in separate bedrooms.

23

Bathrooms

Make sure you fill the paper roll if you finish it, clean before you for health reasons and after you for social reasons. Do not forget to lower the lid!

Need to find out where the restrooms are? Pay attention to what they are called where you are — lots of euphemisms are used to designate that place. You can always ask, "Where can I wash my hands?"

24

When You Are the Host

It is your duty to make sure your guests have a good time. Make sure you know about their eating habits, their conversational taboos, etc.

If you are going to join the social clubs, it is a good idea to keep notes—from the "that was a great idea" to the "never do that again" list.

Make sure your guests know the time and place to go, how to dress, and how long the event may last.

Confirm before the event; it is a good reminder for them and may avoid any last-minute surprises.

If you have a few people over, make sure they get along; you may let them know who is coming, for it takes only one guest to ruin an entire evening.

Do not forget to invite the spouse or the companion.

Greet your guests at the door, and make sure that you take care of their coats, give them a drink, and introduce them to someone before greeting the next guest. Give some information on the person, not only their names, said clearly, but also their relationship with you. If you know they have something in common, engage the conversation on that subject before leaving them.

49

If you are alone as host, enroll the help of a friend.

If someone brings you a present, you may open it in front of your guest but discreetly so as not to embarrass your other guests, who may not have brought something or may have given you an object of lesser value. If it is flowers, put them in a vase and bring them to the room; if it is wine, serve it; if it is chocolate, offer it at the end of the meal.

It is not always necessary for guests to bring a gift; they may show their appreciation by returning your invitation later.

As a host, you are the energy of the party. Think ahead and come up with some fill-in subjects: houses, vacation, films, books, theater, shows, hobbies, travel.

Avoid gossiping.

If there is a problem between two guests, it is your job to take care of it by changing the subject. Use any method to diffuse the tension before it goes too far.

And finally, when the time comes to get rid of your guests—an hour after the hot drink, more or less—start giving hints: offer juices, mention discreetly your early day at work, take advantage of someone leaving to ask if someone else needs a taxi.

When having people sleeping over at your house, make sure that you have towels for them, and if you must enter their rooms, knock first and wait for an answer, even if it is your house.

25

Neighbors

If you are having a party at your house, warn your neighbors ahead of time. A box of chocolate after may smooth things out before your next party.

If you move into a place, it is a good idea to go and introduce yourself or invite your neighbors over.

26

Castles

Castles are expensive to maintain; if you're lucky enough to be invited to one, don't expect the rooms to be well heated or air-conditioned, or to have loads of hot water. Bring clothes accordingly. It is customary to give a tour to the guests. Show interest, even if feigned; ask questions about the history of the place. You are only asked to show polite interest, but interest and respect you must show.

27

Driving

You may be a great driver, but how many do you think there are like you on the road? Use turn signals, and drive accordingly. The truth is that you are responsible for the people in your car, and of those in other cars. Open the door for a lady passenger and help her in and out of the car. When you drive her back, accompany her to the door or at least wait till she has entered the building before taking off.

28

Presents

It is always a nice gesture when invited to come with a little present. It can be flowers, a box of chocolate, or, if specifically requested, dessert. A bottle of wine may be appropriate, but check with your host so that you know which one to bring and from which price range.

Do not forget to remove the price or cover it with a label.

If you're invited to a wedding or another important celebration, you may want to send a present even if you're unable to attend.

Roses should always be given in odd numbers.

"Your mom knit it herself."

29

Jewels

Nothing ostentatious, and do take care not to lose them when you're staying somewhere; otherwise you risk an embarrassing situation. Make sure you have a safe place to keep them.

Now you are ready to go out
and into the social light; you have enough
information to dive in. Do not fret or worry
about forgetting a rule, since they are not set in
stone but tend to change with time and place.
Just watch and learn, and always be kind.
Kindness will open many doors. If you
understand that simple philosophy, you will
always land on your feet. Enjoy, have fun, and let
your light shine!